UKRAINE

A New Independence

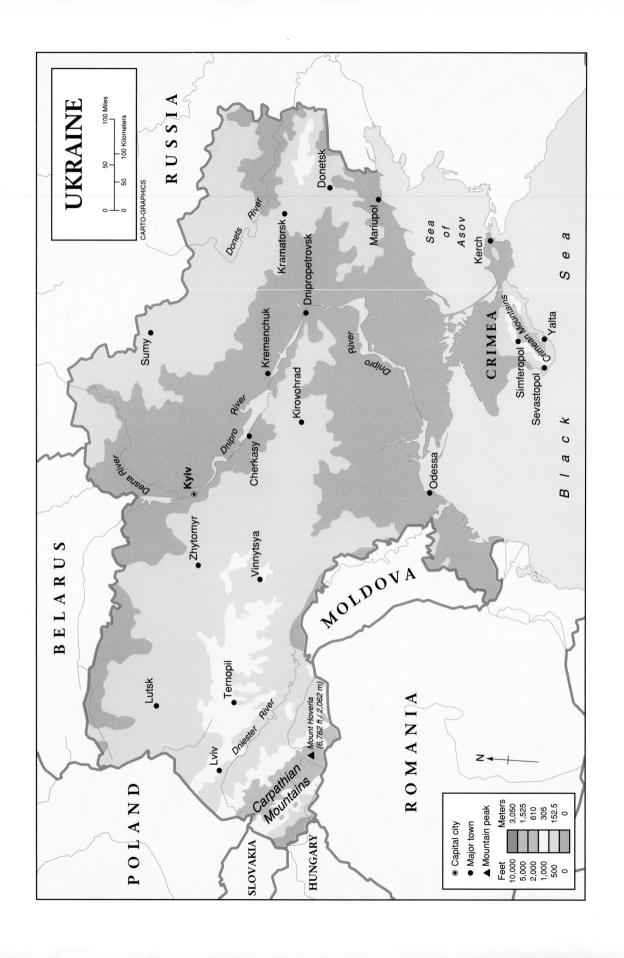

FEB 4 1997

EXPLORING CULTURES OF THE WORLD

UKRAINE

A New Independence

Rebecca Clay

3 1120 01876 5783
j 947.71 C621 uk
Clay, Rebecca.
Ukraine

BENCHMARK BOOKS

MARSHALL CAVENDISH

NEW YORK

With thanks to the people at St. Michael's Ukrainian Catholic Church and the Ukrainian Heritage Center in New Haven, Connecticut, for their expert review of the manuscript.

Benchmark Books
Marshall Cavendish Corporation
99 White Plains Road
Tarrytown, New York 10591-9001

© Marshall Cavendish Corporation 1997

All rights reserved. No part of this book may be reproduced or utilized in any form or by any means electronic or mechanical including photocopying, recording, or by any information storage and retrieval system, without permission from the copyright holders.

Library of Congress Cataloging-in-Publication Data
Clay, Rebecca.
    Ukraine : a new independence / Rebecca Clay.
        p.   cm. — (Exploring cultures of the world)
    Includes bibliographical references.
    Summary: Discusses the geography, history, people, and culture of this rich and fertile nation, which struggled for centuries to be independent and now faces the challenges of its freedom.
    ISBN 0-7614-0334-5 (lib. binding)
    1. Ukraine—Juvenile literature.   [1. Ukraine.]   I. Title. II. Series.
DK508.12.C57   1997
947' .71—dc20
                                                96-19002
                                                  CIP
                                                    AC

Printed in Hong Kong

Front cover: Two Ukrainian women play traditional instruments.
Back cover: Swallow's Nest in Yalta

Photo Credits
Front cover: ©Alex Borodulin/Leo de Wys, Inc.; back cover: Leo de Wys, Inc.; title page and pages 24–25: ©IFA Bilderteam/Leo de Wys, Inc.; pages 6, 52: Photos courtesy of the Ukrainian Heritage Center, New Haven, Connecticut; pages 8, 12: North Wind Picture Archives; pages 11, 26: ©Krzysztof Wojcik/Gamma Liaison; pages 14, 41: ©Jeff Greenberg/dMRp/Photo Researchers, Inc.; page 16: ©Novosti/Gamma Liaison; page 17: ©Tony Stone Images, Inc.; pages 18, 22: ©Bob Stern/Gamma Liaison; pages 20, 30, 35: ©David Kampfner/Liaison International; page 27: Leo de Wys, Inc.; page 32: Ria-Novosti/Sovfoto/PNI; page 34: Bruce Dale/©National Geographic Society Image Collection; page 37: ©Arthur Hustwitt/Leo de Wys, Inc.; pages 38–39, 55: ©W. Hille/Leo de Wys, Inc.; page 42: ©Andy Levin/Photo Researchers, Inc.; pages 44, 50: ©Jeff Greenberg/dMRp/International Stock Photo; page 46: Steve Raymer/©National Geographic Society Image Collection; page 47: ©Olympia/Gamma Liaison; page 48: ©Peter Symasko/International Stock Photo; page 54: ©S. Oristaglio/Photo Researchers, Inc.

The Mitten was adapted from *The Mitten, A Ukranian Folktale*, copyright ©1989 by Jan Brett. Reprinted by permission of G.P. Putnam's Sons.

Contents

The poet Taras Shevchenko wrote of independence for Ukraine.

1
GEOGRAPHY AND HISTORY

The Struggle
to Be Free

Love your Ukraine,
Love her . . . in the harshest time.
In the very last harsh minute
Pray to God for her.

*W*hen the poet and painter who wrote these beautiful words died
in 1861, he was so loved by his people that Ukrainians often
visited his burial place. He inspired the people of Ukraine to love the
richness of their language and to dream of freedom for their country.
Today, he is a national hero, and streets, avenues, ships, and museums throughout the land are named for him.

His name was Taras Shevchenko, and his life began in poverty,
misery, and sadness. He was born in 1814 into a family of serfs—
laborers who were bound to the land and forced to serve a wealthy
landowner. At the time, Ukraine was part of Russia, and many
Ukrainians were serfs. In the system of serfdom, whole families of

7

serfs were legally and economically tied to the land, sometimes for generations. Landowners became very rich through this system. Serfs, however, owned nothing. They were not even free to leave the landowner's estate. Shevchenko's parents died while he was young, and he had to serve the landowner as a houseboy. When he was fourteen, he ran away from the landowner, who had been cruel to him.

In the countryside, a different, kinder landowner took him in. Shevchenko was lucky; this man made sure the teenager learned to read and write. He could also see that Shevchenko had artistic

Ukrainian serfs had very hard lives. Although they were not slaves, serfs could not own their own land.

talent, so he took him along on visits to great European cities, which were filled with fine works of art. Later, in St. Petersburg, in western Russia, Shevchenko entered the St. Petersburg Academy of Art to study painting.

Despite his good fortune, Shevchenko dreamed of being free. Finally, in 1838, when he was twenty-four years old, an artist friend in St. Petersburg gave him enough money to buy his freedom.

While Shevchenko was painting in St. Petersburg, he also began to write poems about life in the Ukrainian villages of his childhood. He published his first collection of poems in 1840 while living in Russia. A year later, Shevchenko published a long poem criticizing the Russian czars, or rulers, for their poor treatment of Ukrainian people. He also began to paint and exhibit pictures describing the fate of Ukraine when the Russian czars introduced serfdom.

When he returned to Ukraine in 1846, Shevchenko was shocked to see how poor the people were. He joined a secret group and wrote poems criticizing Nicholas I, the Russian czar, who still ruled Ukraine. When the czar found out, Shevchenko was arrested. He was sent to a military fort in Siberia, a vast, cold, desolate region in Russia. The fort was like a prison. Shevchenko was forced to serve as a soldier there for ten years. He was forbidden to write or paint, but he found a way to do both secretly.

After his release in 1857, Shevchenko was not allowed to live in Ukraine again. But he was permitted to visit, and during one trip, he was arrested again. This time, the czar forced him to leave Ukraine forever. He was never allowed to visit his homeland again. He spent the rest of his life in St. Petersburg. After his death in 1861, however, Shevchenko's body was returned to Ukraine. He was buried high on a hill above his favorite river, the Dnipro. Today, Ukrainians still remember the poet and painter who inspired them to achieve their dream of freedom and independence.

On the Border

It would not be until 1991—well over a century after Shevchenko's death—that Ukraine would be free. (There was a brief period from 1918–1921 when Ukraine was independent.) To understand this nation's long struggle, we need to look at Ukraine's place in history and its location on the European continent.

The word Ukraine (you-CRANE) means "borderland." It was named this because the region was once the easternmost territory of the Polish Empire, located along the empire's border with Russia. In the 1700s, the Russians helped free the Ukrainians from Poland. Ukraine then became part of the Russian Empire. In 1917, revolutionary Russians overthrew the czar and set up a new system of government. Russia then became the most important republic, or state, in an enormous country called the Union of Soviet Socialist Republics (USSR), or the Soviet Union. Ukraine was another very important republic in the Soviet Union.

In the 1980s, the Soviet Union began to fall apart. Many Ukrainians then worked hard to make their country independent. In 1991, after centuries of struggle, Ukraine declared its independence.

A Rich, Fertile Land

Ukraine is located in southeastern Europe, north of the Black Sea. It is almost as big as the state of Texas. Much of the land is covered with flat, fertile plains called steppes (STEPS). These plains are blanketed with a rich black soil called chernozem. This soil makes Ukraine one of the best farming regions in Europe.

Ukraine has two mountainous areas. The Carpathian Mountains are in the southwest corner of the country. The

Ukraine's rich soil makes it one of the best farming areas in Europe.

Carpathians are dotted with pine trees and alpine meadows. Pretty villages are tucked into the rolling hills. The Crimean Mountains are a chain of low, rocky mountains that seem to rise out of the Black Sea, in the south. Many Ukrainians love to hike in the mountains and look for mushrooms and berries.

Ukraine has three major rivers—the Dnipro, Dniester, and Donets. The Dnipro is the third-largest river in all of Europe. The Dnipro is a national symbol of pride in Ukraine. Over the years, many artists have been inspired to write about it, paint pictures of it, and compose music about it.

11

An Ancient Civilization

The Trypillians were the first farmers that we know of in Ukraine. They lived between 4,000 and 6,000 years ago. The Trypillians lived in long, rectangular log houses. They grew wheat and raised animals for food.

Little is known of the early history of Ukraine, because no records were kept. But many experts believe that the ancient Ukrainians were called the "Rus." In the late fifth century, a village grew up along the Dnipro River about 600 miles from

In A.D. 988, Prince Volodymyr brought Christianity to the region around the city of Kyiv.

the Black Sea. It was called Kyiv (key-EHV), and it soon became the center of a region called Kyivan Rus.

Kyiv was a busy port city. Merchant ships carried cargo along the Dnipro between the Baltic and Black Seas. Its location soon made Kyiv a major political and cultural center. People from distant lands traveled there to trade their products and ideas.

Over the centuries, many different groups of peoples settled throughout Kyivan Rus. In 988, Prince Volodymyr tried to bring all of the groups together under one religion. He forced everyone to accept the Christian faith.

When Prince Volodymyr died, his son, Yaroslav the Wise, became the ruler of Kyivan Rus. By then, it was the largest state in all of Europe. But when Yaroslav died, there was no strong leader to take his place. The state began to break apart. In the early 1200s, it was invaded by Tatars, warriors from central Asia. Many people in Kyivan Rus fled to Poland, where they became serfs.

The Cossacks

The region was now filled with many different invaders—Turks, Tatars, Poles, and Russians. Finally, a group of peasants decided to fight the invaders. They created their own army, and they were known as the Cossacks. The word *cossack* (KAH-zak) means "adventurer" or "free person." The Cossacks developed a reputation as fierce fighters. They called their leaders hetmans.

The most famous Cossack hetman in Ukrainian history is Bohdan Khmelnitsky. He managed to free Ukraine from Polish rule in 1648. The Poles had conquered much of Ukraine in 1569. But independence lasted only a few years.

A statue of the famous Cossack leader Bohdan Khmelnitsky stands in Kyiv.

The Russians had helped the Cossacks in their struggle against Poland, and they forced Ukraine to become part of the Russian Empire. During the 1800s, the region became known as Ukraine, a province of Russia.

The Soviet Era (1917-1991)

After the Russian Revolution of 1917, Ukraine became one of the republics of the new Soviet Union. In the Soviet Union, a new system of government—communism—was set up. Under communism, individuals are not permitted to own private property or to work for personal gain. Instead, everyone is supposed to work for the good of the nation. In this way, Communists believe, poverty will disappear and all people will live as equals. Under the Communist system, the government is all-powerful.

Ukrainians tried to resist becoming part of the Soviet Union. In 1918, Ukrainian independence was gained, but only for three years.

During the 1930s, the Soviet Union's leader Joseph Stalin began to turn Ukraine's privately owned farms into collectives. These were large farms, owned and run by the government.

By this time, Ukraine had long been a very important agricultural region. Ukraine was indeed the "breadbasket of Europe," as the land came to be known. Its products were shipped throughout the Soviet Union. The profits from its farms, however, did not belong to Ukrainians. Instead, they belonged to the Soviet state.

The system of serfdom had ended in 1861. Ukrainians had been free for many years to own their own farms. Now they resented losing them and tried to resist collectivization. This was a dark period in Ukrainian history. Stalin had all the grain taken away from farmers and created a famine. As many as 10 million people died.

Stalin also forbade Ukrainians from practicing many of their traditional customs. They were not even allowed to write their own language.

In the late 1970s and early 1980s, the Soviet Union's economy began to suffer. In 1985, Mikhail Gorbachev became the Soviet leader. He hoped to improve conditions by relaxing many of the stricter government policies. His policy of perestroika (per-uh-STROY-kuh) was meant to bring about a better economic system. Some people began to open their own, private businesses. Gorbachev also allowed people greater personal and political freedoms. This policy was called glasnost (GLAZ-nohst). As a result, Ukrainians were able to revive some traditions, such as using the Ukrainian language in their schools. They, like other Soviets, were allowed more freedom to criticize the government.

Perestroika and glasnost gave Ukrainians the confidence to start pressing once again for freedom and independence. In 1989, some Ukrainians created Rukh, a political party for democracy. On January 21, 1990, 300,000 Ukrainian men,

The changes that President Mikhail Gorbachev brought to the Soviet government allowed Ukrainians to move toward democracy.

Private businesses began during Gorbachev's rule. Today they are springing up all over Ukraine, even on the sidewalks. Here, a woman samples cosmetics from a vendor.

women, and children held hands in a very long line to show that they no longer wanted to be ruled by the Soviet government. Every day, Ukraine was getting closer to independence.

Free at Last

In August 1991, members of Gorbachev's government tried to remove him from his position as president. This event showed the world that the Soviet government was in deep trouble. Ukraine took advantage of the unstable situation

A fierce spirit of independence made Ukrainians struggle for self-government. At this rally in Kyiv, a man holds a trident—the Ukrainian national emblem.

UKRAINIAN GOVERNMENT

Ukraine is a republic made up of twenty-four oblasts, or administrative regions. The central government has three branches: the executive, the judicial, and the legislative.

The executive branch is the office of the president. The people of Ukraine elect a president every five years. A president may serve for only two terms in a row.

Ukraine's legislative, or law-making, branch is the Supreme Council, which is also called the Parliament. The Supreme Council is made up of one chamber, or house, which has 450 deputies, or representatives. Each deputy is elected to a four-year term. The judicial branch is made up of the Supreme Court.

Since official independence on December 1, 1991, at least forty political parties have been created in Ukraine. The Parliament includes members from many of these different parties. The largest parties are the People's Movement of Ukraine (Rukh), the Communist party, the Socialist party, the Peasants' party, the Democratic party, and the Republican party.

and declared itself independent of the Soviet Union. Because the Soviet government was too weak to resist, Ukraine won its freedom. At the end of 1991, the Soviet Union collapsed and ceased to exist.

Despite its independence, Ukraine still faces great challenges. Ukraine must learn to govern its own people now. It also must find ways to improve its economy. More new, privately owned businesses are being created every day.

Ukrainians are learning how to meet these political and economic challenges. They are hopeful that they will succeed. Ukraine is blessed with rich and fertile lands. And Ukrainians feel the lively spirit and optimism of a people for whom freedom was long in coming.

These women work on a large farm in Ukraine. Agriculture is one of the most important industries in the country.

2
THE PEOPLE

From Fertile Fields to Busy Streets

Ukraine is a crowded country with more than 52 million people. Thirty-seven million are ethnic Ukrainians, which means their roots in Ukraine go back hundreds of years and many generations. The second-largest ethnic group is Russian, with about 11 million people. There are also many smaller groups, including those whose families moved into Ukraine from nearby countries such as Belarus, Poland, Hungary, and Romania.

Most Ukrainians are well educated and work hard. They belong to many different professions, including farming, mining, medicine, teaching, and science. In the big cities, many work in factories—building machines, welding metals, or manufacturing chemicals. Ukraine also has many artists, such as writers, musicians, painters, dancers, and actors. In addition, some Ukrainians are businesspeople. They own stores

At an outdoor market in the city of Lviv, a woman sells carrots, beets, radishes, and other locally grown produce.

and shops, providing services such as cutting hair, sewing clothes, and selling books. Others own factories, restaurants, and other businesses.

Many people are miners. Mining is a big business in Ukraine. Huge amounts of coal, clay, marble, salt, and other important materials are extracted from the land. There are also many farmers. In the rich fields of the vast steppes, they grow a great variety of grains and vegetables. Ukrainian farmers are lucky because so much of their land is covered with chernozem. This fertile soil allows them to grow such crops as wheat, corn, sugar beets, potatoes, rye, and fruit. Other farm products, like sunflowers, flax, tobacco, and wine grapes, are important, too. Farmers also raise cattle, sheep, poultry, pigs, and goats.

It is still quite common in Ukraine to see farm families riding along country roads in horse-drawn carts. They bring their fresh produce and meat to the cities, where they sell them in shops and outdoor stalls.

Cathedrals and Sailing Ships

Most of Ukraine's large cities are located in the central and eastern parts of the country, along the Dnipro and Donets Rivers. During the Soviet era, factories and mines were built in or near cities. Many of the factories are still running. They make a great variety of products for consumers and industry.

Kyiv is the capital city. More than 2.6 million people live in this ancient, beautiful city sprawling alongside the Dnipro. Rich with history, Kyiv's skyline is dotted with the glittering golden domes of its many churches and cathedrals. Throughout Kyiv, both wide boulevards and narrow streets are lined with large shade trees. There are quiet parks and gardens, too, where adults can relax and children can play. Archaeologists—people who study the settlements of ancient peoples—believe that Kyiv is at least 1,500 years old. It began as a village in A.D. 482. It was built up as a fortress in the 600s.

Kyiv has been attacked many times in its long history. It was destroyed in 1240 by the invading Tatars. In the 1940s, during World War II, the city was almost destroyed by both German and Soviet armies. Fortunately, however, many of Kyiv's ancient churches and buildings were not bombed.

Kyiv's skyline is a blend of ancient and modern buildings.

Today, Kyiv is a thriving center. Every day, trucks from Ukraine's farms and factories bring fresh produce and products into the city. Several times a week, Kyivans head to huge outdoor markets to buy groceries.

Beach-goers flock to the Crimean Peninsula's Black Sea coast for sun and surf.

Ukraine's main seaport is Odessa, located on the Black Sea. It is also a resort city much loved by vacationers. A settlement may have existed on this site as long ago as the 300s. Today, Odessa is home to people from many different national origins. The population is mostly made up of Ukrainians, Russians, Bulgarians, and Moldovans. Here they enjoy the city's sandy beaches and its exciting cultural life. Odessa is a port city, and many of its residents build ships for a living.

Yalta is a popular holiday and resort town on the Crimean Peninsula, on the Black Sea. Russian czars and nobility often went there for beach vacations. In February 1945, toward the end of World War II, several world leaders met in Yalta to discuss the fate of the soon-to-be defeated Germany. One of those leaders was the American president Franklin D. Roosevelt. A street in Yalta was named Roosevelt Avenue to honor him. Yalta is also famous for producing fine wines and canned fruit.

The Swallow's Nest in Yalta sits high on a cliff above the Black Sea. It was built in the early 1900s to look like a medieval castle.

SAY IT IN UKRAINIAN

Here is how you say some common words and phrases in Ukrainian:

добрий ранок   (DOH-bray RAH-nok): Good morning.
добрий денъ   (DOH-bray dehn): Good afternoon.
добрий вечір   (DOH-bray VEH-cheer): Good evening.
як живеш?   (yak zhi-VESH): How are you?
дуже добре   (DOO-zheh DO-breh): Very well.
привіт   (prih-VEET): Hi!
що нового?   (shcho no-VO-ho): What's new?

A proverb in Ukrainian:

Мова—це душа народу.   Language is the soul of a nation.
(MO-vah—tseh doo-SHAH nah-RO-doo).

In 1256, the Ukrainian king Danylo (Daniel) Ramonovych Halytsky founded the city of Lviv, in western Ukraine. He named it after his son Prince Lev, or Leo. Located near the Polish border, Lviv was once part of Poland. Lviv is a beautiful city. Its old neighborhoods are crisscrossed with narrow cobblestone streets, parks, and outdoor cafés. Today, thousands of students attend its many colleges and universities.

A Different Alphabet

Most Ukrainians speak both Ukrainian and Russian. These two languages have many similar words. Each uses a slightly different version of a form of writing called the Cyrillic alphabet. The Cyrillic alphabet was first developed by St. Cyril, a Christian missionary who combined Greek letters and some Hebrew symbols.

A few of the thirty-three letters in the Ukrainian version of the Cyrillic alphabet look and sound almost like English letters, such as *k*, *m*, *t*, *a*, *e*, and *o*. Other letters sound similar but look very different. For example, б is *b*, ц is *ts*, ф is *f*, and

28

ч is *ch*. The Ukrainian language is tricky for English-speakers because some letters look familiar but do not sound at all the same. *B*, for example, sounds like *v*; *c* like *s*; and *p* like *r*.

Going to Worship

Most Ukrainians belong to one of several Christian religious groups. There are also smaller numbers of people who follow Islam, Judaism, and Buddhism. In all, more than sixty variations of different religious faiths are practiced in Ukraine.

During the Soviet era, all religions were banned, and most churches, synagogues (Jewish houses of worship), and mosques (Muslim houses of worship) were closed. Many people were forced to worship secretly. But since Ukraine won its independence in 1991, all people have been allowed to worship openly and freely.

In 1988, Christianity in Ukraine celebrated its 1,000th birthday. Today, the most popular Christian faith is Ukrainian Orthodox. Thirty-five million Ukrainians attend the Ukrainian Orthodox Church, making it the largest religious denomination, or group, in the country. Many Orthodox churches have cupolas, special roofs that are shaped like pears. The walls are decorated with colorful designs of flowers.

The second-largest denomination is the Ukrainian Greek-Catholic Church, with about 5 million people, mostly living in the western regions. Ukrainian Russians, who mostly live along the Russian border, attend the Russian Orthodox Church. It can be difficult to tell the difference between these churches because so many of their ceremonies are similar.

Some Orthodox and Greek-Catholic church services last for many hours, sometimes all day. People come and go whenever they like. There are no benches, so all the worshipers stand.

A Christian church in rural Ukraine is elaborately decorated. Most Ukrainians are Christians.

Sometimes a choir will sing, but there are no musical instruments to accompany the singers. When a church is crowded, people may listen to the service on loudspeakers outside.

In recent years, some Ukrainians have become interested in religions brought from western Europe and North America. People who follow the Baptist, Lutheran, and Mormon faiths have been preaching to Ukrainians, for example. They are teaching Christian concepts that are quite different from those of the Orthodox faiths.

A Trident, Flag, and National Song

Today, Ukrainians have three symbols that represent their courageous struggle to be free of foreign rule. One, the trident, was created almost 1,800 years ago in Ukraine. It looks like a three-pronged spear. At one time, it was used on gold and silver coins and on the doors of cathedrals and palaces. During the Soviet era, it was forbidden to show the trident. But when Ukraine achieved independence, the trident was revived and became the national emblem.

Ukraine now has its own flag as well. For most of the country's history, the flags of other states flew over Ukraine. The official flag of independent Ukraine is a simple traditional design. The top half is blue, and the bottom half is yellow. Some people believe that the blue represents the sky and the yellow represents golden wheat or sunflowers.

The third symbol is Ukraine's national anthem. It is called "Ukraine Is Not Yet Dead." The song expresses the great hope and desire of the Ukrainian people to be free. It also speaks of the luck the people will need to "live happily in our land."

Ukraine Is Not Yet Dead

Ukraine is not yet dead, nor its glory and freedom,
Luck will yet smile on us brother Ukrainians.
Our enemies will die, as the dew does in the sunshine,
and, we, brothers, we'll live happily in our land.
We'll not spare either our souls or bodies to get freedom
and we'll prove that we brothers are of Kozak kin.
We'll rise up, brothers, all of us, from the Sian to the Don.
We won't let anyone govern in our motherland.
The Black Sea will smile yet, grandfather Dnipro will rejoice,
In our Ukraine luck will be high.
Our persistence, our sincere toil will prove its rightness,
and our freedom's loud song will spread throughout Ukraine.
It'll reflect upon the Carpathians, will sound through the steppes,
and Ukraine's glory will rise among the people.

Four people in traditional clothing raise long horns to sound the start of a folk festival in the Carpathian Mountains.

3

FAMILY LIFE, FESTIVALS, AND FOOD

Living and Playing Together

Many Ukrainian families live in apartments located in cities and towns. During the Soviet era, many huge apartment buildings were erected by the government. They are still used today. Inside, the apartments are often small, with one to four rooms. Some Ukrainian families also have a small house, or dacha, in the countryside. They go there to rest, to play, and to grow flowers and vegetables.

Some Ukrainian families live year-round in the countryside, in colorful dachas surrounded by flower gardens. These rural homes do not always have indoor plumbing. Most dachas have wood-burning stoves to provide warmth during Ukraine's cold winters.

Ukrainian families are closely knit. Family members live near one another and spend much of their free time together. Adults often remain close to their parents, brothers, and sisters. They also have good relationships with their in-laws—the parents, brothers, and sisters of their husbands or wives.

In these extended families, people celebrate holidays and important occasions together.

Today, most immediate families are small, with two parents and one or two children. Children are not often spoiled, and they are taught to be "seen but not heard." They are usually well behaved, and they respect their parents and help around the house. When they grow up, children are expected to take care of their aging parents.

Because there is not always enough housing in Ukraine, three or four generations may live together in the same apartment. Children may live with their parents, grandparents, and great-grandparents.

Some families have small, colorfully painted dachas in the countryside where they can rest and enjoy one another's company.

Ukrainian families generally spend much of their time together.

Women usually take care of the children. They also cook and clean. At home, men are responsible for maintenance work, such as fixing cars or televisions. Husbands also help out with the shopping. It is often necessary to visit many shops to get all the products that the family needs.

For the Church, Women, and Soldiers

Most holidays and festivals celebrate religious occasions. Christmas, Easter, and Epiphany (the celebration of the day the three Wise Men visited the infant Jesus) are especially

MAKIVNYK: UKRAINIAN POPPY SEED CAKE (A CHRISTMASTIME TREAT)

Preheat oven to 350°F. Butter two medium loaf pans.

Ingredients:

3/4 cup poppy seeds
1 cup milk
1/2 pound (2 sticks) butter
1 1/3 cups light brown sugar
3 eggs
1/2 teaspoon vanilla
1 teaspoon lemon rind

Sift together:

2 cups unbleached flour
3 teaspoons baking powder
1/2 teaspoon salt

1. Heat poppy seeds and milk in a saucepan. Remove from heat just before the mixture starts to boil. Let it stand until it reaches room temperature.
2. Cream the butter with the sugar. Add the eggs, one at a time, and beat well after adding each.
3. Add the sifted dry ingredients. Stir in the vanilla and lemon rind.
4. Bake in the well-greased loaf pans for 40 to 50 minutes or until a toothpick comes out clean.

important religious celebrations for Christian Ukrainians. Special feasts are prepared for most Christian holidays as well as for New Year's Day.

Ukrainian holidays are usually celebrated on dates from the Old Style, or Julian, calendar, which is thirteen days behind the Gregorian calendar used today. That means that Christmas is celebrated on January 7, not December 25. The Orthodox New Year comes on January 14.

Many Ukrainians start the Christmas celebration when a family member spots the first star in the sky on Christmas Eve, January 6. Then the whole family sits down to a special supper of twelve dishes, including *kutia* (koot-YAH), boiled wheat with honey, and *uzvar* (OOZ-vahr), stewed fruit. Everyone in the family must taste all twelve dishes.

Carolers can be heard on Christmas Eve, Christmas Day, or the day after Christmas. In the past, only boys were allowed to carol in public, and girls could sing along while watching from a window. But today, many girls join the carolers and stroll through the streets singing traditional Christmas songs.

On Christmas Day, married couples go to the home of one of their parents. They are greeted in the doorway, and welcomed with a pot of *kutia*. The day after Christmas is often called the feast of the Mother of God. This is when older

A Ukrainian girl plays the tsymbaly *during a celebration.*

Folk dancers in traditional costume perform in Kyiv.

women are given special attention, with warm greetings and gifts.

Ukrainians mark two Independence Days. One is August 24, when the republic declared its independence from the Soviet Union in 1991. The other is January 22, the day Ukrainian leaders declared independence in 1918. On March 8, Ukrainian women celebrate International Women's Day by having their husbands and sons cook and clean for them. On May 9, big parades mark Victory in Europe Day—the day when World War II ended in Europe in 1945.

Ukrainian festivals are great fun, with men, women, and children singing and dancing for hours. Throughout Ukraine, there are many choirs and dance groups that perform at festivals. Folk dancers often dress in traditional blouses and skirts decorated with hand-done embroidery. Some festivals also feature competitions in which musicians show off how well they play the *bandura* (ban-DOO-ra), the traditional Ukrainian stringed instrument. Other musicians blow into the *trembita* (trem-BEE-ta), a long wooden tube that produces a sad, muffled sound. *Tsymbaly* (tsim-BAH-lee), a stringed instrument, is also played.

Land of Bread and Potatoes

Ukrainian bread is delicious. It is very popular throughout Europe. Bread is so important in Ukraine that people like to offer their favorite guests a loaf of bread, with a small pile of salt on top, as a token of their esteem. Bread is always served at important family events, such as weddings, births of children, and funerals. Some Ukrainians believe that bread is holy and is a gift from God.

Each region of Ukraine has its own special breads, and today there are hundreds of different kinds. One of the most common types is sour rye. Ukrainian bakers also make special breads for festivals, such as loaves filled with cheese, meat, or plums, or breads shaped into braids, called *kolach* (KOH-lak).

The most popular vegetables in Ukraine are beets, cabbage, cucumbers, potatoes, tomatoes, onions, and beans. Cooks combine these delicious vegetables with garlic, dill, and vinegar to make dishes that people have enjoyed for hundreds of years.

Potatoes are served everywhere in Ukraine. They are often added to such favorite soups as borsch (BORSCH), which is made with beets. Sometimes potatoes are grated and shaped into pancakes, which are fried and eaten with cheese or sour cream.

Next to potatoes, cabbage is the most popular vegetable. Cabbage soup is a favorite dish. Cabbage is also used to fill dumplings called *varenyky* (va-REH-neh-keh). Ukrainians also like to stuff cabbage leaves with buckwheat, rice, or meat, and then roll them up.

The most popular meat is pork. Ukrainians especially like ham, bacon, and sausage called *kovbasa* (kohv-bas-AH). Sometimes they grind up the pork to make patties, like

A woman enjoys a lunch of borsch and varenyky *at a restaurant in Lviv. Sour cream is served on the side.*

hamburgers. Ukrainians also like chicken. One popular dish is chicken baked in sour cream and served with potatoes and mushrooms. Chicken Kiev is an international dish that was named after Ukraine's capital city. It is made of chicken breasts stuffed with butter, rolled in flour, and deep fried.

Dairy products are very important in Ukraine. Noodles and *varenyky* are often boiled in milk. Ukrainians also enjoy drinking soured milk. Sour cream is a favorite dairy product. It is often used as a dressing for vegetables, especially tomatoes and cucumbers.

41

Two Ukrainian girls in Odessa on their way to school

4
SCHOOL AND RECREATION

Healthy Body,
Healthy Mind

Most Ukrainian children start nursery school as early as age one, and kindergarten starts at age five. Children start first grade at age six.

All students attend school through the seventh grade. At that time, a student may either go to a trade school or continue through the tenth grade. After that, a student may go to an institute or university.

There are few discipline problems in Ukrainian schools. All students are expected to respect and obey their teachers and professors. Students are not allowed to question the authority of adults. Children are expected to get good grades and to do their homework carefully every night.

Students must take a special exam in order to attend an institute or university. At an institute, they may train to be specialists, such as doctors, engineers, pharmacists, veterinarians, and teachers. Because there are many mines and

These schoolchildren in Lviv are studying English.

factories in Ukraine, there is also a great need for workers skilled in mining, welding, assembly work, and other manufacturing tasks. An institute can prepare young people for such jobs as well.

Many students choose to go to a large university where they can get a broader education. At a university, they may study math, biology, foreign languages, history, literature, and art. Students spend five to six years at a university. When they are finished, they are given a diploma that allows them to work in a specific profession, such as engineering or dentistry. Rather than start work right away, some students prefer to stay at a university and continue to study in a specific field. This usually takes three years.

During the Soviet era, classes were taught in Russian and instructors had to teach Communist history and ideas. Today, Ukrainian is the language of instruction and the country is rediscovering its own past and heroes. Textbooks are being rewritten to teach children about Ukrainian history and customs.

Sports Palaces

In a healthy body, a healthy mind.

—a Ukrainian proverb

Before the 1900s, only rich Ukrainians were active in sports, such as hunting bear, capturing wild horses, running, dancing, and wrestling. The Cossacks' favorite sport was training for combat, such as shooting guns or fighting with swords. During the Soviet era, however, more Ukrainians began to participate in sports.

Sports were an important part of life in the Soviet Union and remain so in Ukraine today. The Soviet government built a sports palace in every city. A sports palace is a place where people can get together for a wide variety of activities, from ice skating to gymnastics. The largest sports palace in Ukraine is in Kyiv.

From 1923 to 1991, Ukrainian athletes competed as part of the Soviet Union's teams at the Olympic Games. Now, these proud athletes represent their own country. The best young athletes are chosen to train and compete. Many dream of winning a gold medal at the Olympic Games.

Today, Ukrainians play more than fifty different sports. Soccer is one of the most popular team sports for boys and girls. There are hundreds of soccer clubs in Ukraine.

Working out with the hula hoop. From a young age, Ukrainians are taught that physical activity is important.

Ukrainians have loved soccer for at least 200 years. The game was popular among the Cossacks in the eighteenth century. In 1921, the major cities formed soccer teams and played against one another for the national championship. The team Dynamo Kyiv usually wins the national championship. Ukrainian soccer players are considered among the best in the world, playing and winning in international competitions such as the World Cup and the European Cup.

In addition to soccer, gymnastics, fencing, and ice and field hockey, Ukrainian sports include volleyball, tennis, table tennis, motorcycle racing, horseback riding, and wrestling.

OKSANA BAIUL: DANCER ON ICE

To the millions of viewers who watched the 1994 Winter Olympics, the Ukrainian figure skater Oksana Baiul was like a graceful ballerina on ice. Competing against the world's best skaters, she won the top prize: the gold medal. She was just sixteen years old at the time, and hardly anyone had ever heard of her.

Oksana's victory was even more dramatic because of her difficult and painful childhood. She was born in a Ukrainian mill town. Her father abandoned the family when Oksana was two years old. She began to skate at the age of three. Her grandparents died when she was ten, and her mother died when Oksana was thirteen, leaving her an orphan. Then, her skating coach left Ukraine and moved to

Oksana Baiul won the gold medal at the 1994 Olympic Games in Lillehammer, Norway.

Canada. But luckily, Galina Zmievskaya, a world-famous skating coach, agreed to train her. She even made Oksana a member of her family in Odessa. Oksana practiced day and night to prepare for the world skating championships.

When Oksana was fifteen, she won the world title for women's figure skating. At the time, she said, "I skate how I feel. I think it must be a gift from God." A year later, she took home the Olympic gold medal, proof that this Ukrainian had become one of the greatest female figure skaters in the world.

Young and old watch, fascinated, as this circus performer does a complex balancing act.

Ukrainians also participate in track and field, shooting, basketball, skiing, handball, and swimming, either in a pool or at the beach. A new sport in Ukraine is kick boxing, which combines boxing and traditional Eastern martial arts. For those who like competition but not physical sport, chess and checkers are played throughout Ukraine.

The Circus and Puppet Shows

Ukrainians love the circus. Every city with more than 500,000 people has its own circus and permanent circus building. Circus troupes also travel around the country to perform for people in small villages.

Young and old Ukrainians flock to the "big top" to watch performers riding horses bareback, flying from one trapeze to another, walking through air on tightropes, juggling balls of fire, or just clowning around. They tremble as the lion tamer puts his head into the mouth of a lion, and they laugh as the clowns throw pies into one another's faces.

Every large Ukrainian city also has its own puppet theater. Both hand puppets and marionettes are used. They act out fairy tales, such as the story of Pinocchio, or old Ukrainian folk stories. Some Ukrainian puppeteers are so talented that they perform in international festivals.

Community Baths

Another common activity in Ukraine is going to a public bath-house. This is part of the "healthy body, healthy mind" way of life. Long ago, in the days of Kyivan Rus, each family had a special log cabin used only for bathing. Everyone took a bath together. Today, public bathhouses, or saunas, can be found in every city and town. These bathhouses are used more for seeing friends and relaxing than for washing up.

Each bathhouse has a women's section and a men's section. The most popular activity is to sit first in a steaming-hot room. The next step is to hit one's back, legs, and arms lightly with a bunch of wet birch branches. Ukrainians believe this helps the blood circulate better. A quick dive into a pool of icy cold water finishes the bath and leaves people refreshed.

Today, Ukrainians make many of the same kinds of beautiful crafts as they did hundreds of years ago, such as these embroidered fabrics and lacquerware.

5
THE ARTS

Bringing Back Tradition

For hundreds of years, Ukrainian artists and craftspeople were not free to create their traditional arts. Instead, they were forced to paint, write, or sing whatever the Russian czars and, later, the Soviet Communists approved of. But now that the country is independent, Ukraine's rich artistic traditions are coming alive again. Just as the country is free, so are its creative people.

Songs of the People

Ukrainians have been writing and playing folk music—the music of the people—for centuries. Long ago, Ukrainian folk singers often sang about love, the beauty of nature, or peasants working in the fields. They also sang about hard work and honesty and the importance of caring about one another and being unselfish.

On market days and religious holidays, musicians strolled about singing long, patriotic folk songs. These often told the

A Ukrainian boy plays a bandura.

story of the Ukrainian people's struggle against their enemies. At the same time as they sang, the musicians would pluck the strings of *banduras*.

Today, many Ukrainian musicians still play traditional instruments such as the *bandura*. Other musicians blow into the flutelike *sopilka* (so-PEEL-ka) or the ten-foot *trembita*, a hollow wooden tube wrapped with birch bark. These instruments are used in performances at festivals, dances, funerals, and other important events.

Eggs, Stitching, and Pots

Ukrainians are very proud of the beauty and quality of their traditional crafts, some of which date back thousands of years. Today, in nearly every region of the country, artists produce finely embroidered fabrics and weave colorful patterned cloth. They make pottery and hand-painted Easter eggs. And they use ancient techniques to produce beautiful wood carvings.

Many of these fine crafts are decorated with traditional patterns and designs. The same patterns may be used on a rug, bowl, or painted egg. The earliest designs were geometric, such as simple squares and circles. Later, Ukrainian artists painted, shaped, or wove pictures of plants and animals into their crafts. Today, a variety of patterns can be found on all Ukrainian folk art.

Embroidery, the art of sewing delicate designs onto cloth, is the most popular folk art. In the past, each village had its own special embroiderers who were paid to create original patterns. All the cloth in every household was decorated with embroidery, from skirts to tablecloths. Today, most families still have one member who is an expert embroiderer.

Many everyday shirts, blouses, and skirts are still embroidered. Styles vary from region to region, but most include squares, circles, crosses, leaves, and flowers. The designs may feature just a few colors, such as black, red, and yellow, or many colors.

Weavers have been making clothes, carpets, tapestries, and bed coverings for more than 500 years. One of the most popular objects is the *kylym* (key-LEEM). This is a large, colorful carpet made to hang on the wall rather than cover the floor. Some weavers also make *rushnyky* (ROOSH-nehk). These are special towels that may be placed over a basket

DECORATED EASTER EGGS

The ancient art of decorating Easter eggs is called *pysanka* (peh-SANK-ah) painting. *Pysanka* means "written egg" in Ukrainian. Painted Easter eggs celebrate the happy arrival of springtime and new life. A long time ago, people believed that the painted eggs had magical powers and could protect them from bad things, such as getting sick. Some Ukrainian Easter eggs are so beautiful that they are displayed in museums for everyone to enjoy.

Decorating an Easter egg is not an easy job. There are several different methods to choose from. The artist may paint it with a brush, dip it in colored dye, drip hot wax over the surface, or scratch a design into the delicate shell. For a complex design, the artist may use all of these methods for one egg.

Each egg may be dipped in different colored dyes—usually red, white, blue, green, and yellow. Long ago, the dyes came from natural materials, such as plant roots, animal skins, or the bark of special trees. Today, most dyes are synthetic, or artificial. Once it is dyed, the egg is carefully painted with a delicate design, such as a sun, circle, dots, crosses, squiggles, churches, flowers, or leaves.

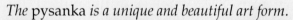
The pysanka *is a unique and beautiful art form.*

Clothes are often still decorated with traditional embroidery.

of food and taken to church for the Easter blessing. A *rushnyky* may also be hung on the wall to cover a cherished icon, which is a religious image. To celebrate weddings, embroiderers design *rushnyky* with joyful symbols and colors.

Ukrainians are also proud of their talent and skill in producing pottery, a craft that their ancestors practiced nearly 6,500 years ago. Pottery is the term for both useful and decorative objects made of different kinds of clay. The potter shapes the clay and then fires, or bakes, it in a kiln (pottery

A UKRAINIAN FOLKTALE: THE MITTEN

Nicki wants his grandmother to knit him a new pair of white woolen mittens. She doesn't want to make the mittens white, however, because if he drops one in the snow, he won't be able to find it. But Nicki only wants white mittens, so she goes ahead and knits him a beautiful pair.

One winter day, Nicki goes out to play and drops one of the mittens in the snow by mistake. He is so busy playing that he doesn't notice it is missing. He heads off to play in the woods.

One by one, the curious animals of the woods find the mitten. First, the mole climbs in to stay warm. Next a snowshoe rabbit squeezes in, then a hedgehog, an owl, a badger, a fox, and a big bear. By then, the mitten is big and fat and bulging with all the animals crowded inside.

Finally, a tiny mouse comes along and sits down on the great bear's nose. Pretty soon, the mouse causes the big bear to let out a huge sneeze. The mitten shoots up into the air and all the animals fly out and run away in all directions.

Just at that moment, Nicki starts for home. He sees the white mitten as it is falling to earth. He catches it just as his grandmother looks out the window to check if he is bringing home both of the white woolen mittens. And he is!

oven) until it becomes hard. Then the object is painted with bright folk-art or modern designs.

Today, colorful bowls, plates, cups, and other pieces of household pottery are sold in markets and shops throughout the country. Some potters also create children's toys, such as small whistles and little cats, sheep, and roosters.

Telling Stories

Like most people, Ukrainians love a good story. Today, both children and adults alike enjoy hearing traditional folktales. As children grow up, the stories that they are told change.

Each age group has its own stories. Babies often listen to their mothers sing them cradle songs. Some sections of a cradle song may sound like a cat purring or a bird singing, to help the babies go to sleep. Their mothers also sing them lullabies, which have more rhythm and different sounds.

As they get a little older, children are told nonsense stories and riddles and are sung counting songs. Counting songs help children learn numbers. Very young children love to hear popular stories such as *Kolobok* ("The Ball") or *Rukavychka* ("The Mitten"). Kids in school like magic stories that tell about being good or bad.

Paintings and Sculpture

Throughout the centuries, Ukrainian artists have welcomed ideas from other nations. They were especially influenced by artists in Greece, Italy, Germany, Poland, and Russia. Ukrainian artists often traveled to the great European cities, such as Paris, France, and Munich, Germany, to study new techniques and methods. But during the Soviet era, painters and sculptors were allowed to work in only one style, called Soviet realism. This style usually depicted huge landscapes or scenes of agricultural or industrial workers. Any artwork that did not conform to Soviet realism was destroyed. Because they had no freedom of expression, many artists left Ukraine to live in other countries.

Now that Ukraine is an independent country, its artists are free to paint or sculpt whatever they wish. Today, there is a revival of Ukrainian fine art. Like many other Ukrainians, artists are enjoying a new era of creativity and energy.

Country Facts

Official Name: YkpaiHa, or Ukraina (Ukraine)

Capital: Kyiv

Location: in central Europe, bordered on the north by Belarus and the north and east by Russia. On the south lie the Black Sea, the Sea of Asov, Moldova, and Romania; and on the west, Hungary, Slovakia, and Poland.

Area: 233,100 square miles (603,730 square kilometers). *Greatest distances:* east–west, 800 miles (1,287 kilometers); north–south, 560 miles (900 kilometers). *Coastline:* 1,073 miles (1,726 kilometers)

Elevation: *Highest:* Mount Hoverla, Carpathian Mountains, 6,762 feet (2,062 meters). *Lowest:* Black Sea, approximately sea level

Climate: moderate continental. Four distinct seasons, with an annual snowfall; coldest in northeast; Mediterranean climate on southern coast of Crimea

Population: 52,000,000. *Distribution:* 67 percent urban; 32 percent rural

Form of Government: republic

Important Products: *Natural Resources:* coal, iron, tin, copper, lead, zinc. *Agriculture:* wheat, barley, buckwheat, corn, millet, oats, beets, cabbage, cucumber, potatoes, tomatoes, apples, pears, plums, berries. *Industries:* oil refining, chemicals, metalworking, machine building, electronics, printing, manufacturing, mining, construction, transportation, and communication

Basic Unit of Money: karbovantsi; 1 karbovantsi = 100 kopeka

Languages: Ukrainian and Russian

Religion: Ukrainian Orthodox; Ukrainian Greek-Catholic; Russian Orthodox

Flag: two horizontal stripes of blue and yellow

National Anthem: *Shche Ne Vmerla Ukraina* ("Ukraine Is Not Yet Dead")

Major Holidays: New Year's Day, January 1; Orthodox New Year (not official), January 14; Christmas, January 7; International Women's Day, March 8; Victory in Europe Day, May 9; Independence Days, January 22 and August 24; and Easter

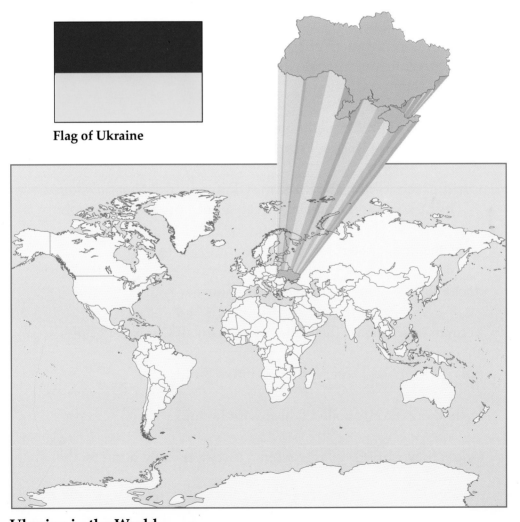

Flag of Ukraine

Ukraine in the World

Glossary

bandura (ban-DOO-ra): a traditional Ukrainian stringed instrument

borsch (BORSCH): a beet soup that may also include potatoes and cabbage

chernozem (chor-NO-zem): a layer of rich black soil on the Ukrainian farmlands

collective: a farm or factory in the Soviet Union that was owned and run by the government

communism: a system of government in which a single, all-powerful government party owns and controls all goods and their production

Cossack (KAH-zak): a Ukrainian peasant who fought for freedom against Russia, Poland, and other enemies

Cyrillic (seh-RI-lik): the Russian/Ukrainian alphabet developed by St. Cyril and featuring Greek letters and Hebrew symbols

czar: the title of the ruler of Russia from 1547 to 1917

dacha (DAH-cheh): a small country house

hetman (HET-man): the leader of an army of Cossack fighters

kolach (KOH-lak): bread shaped into a braid

kutia (koot-YAH): boiled wheat with honey

kylym (key-LEEM): a large woven carpet, usually hung on the wall *pysanka* (peh-SANK-ah): the ancient art of decorating Ukrainian Easter eggs

rushnyky (ROOSH-nehk): embroidered towels used for special occasions

serfs: peasant farmers who were under the control of the landowners and were sold along with the land

sopilka (so-PEEL-ka): a flute-like musical instrument

steppes (STEPS): flat, grassy, mostly treeless meadows

traditional: a long-established way of doing something

trembita (trem-BEE-ta): a long, tube-like musical instrument made from hollowed-out wood and wrapped with birch bark

tsymbaly (tsim-BAH-lee): a stringed musical instrument

uzvar (OOZ-vahr): stewed fruit

varenyky (va-REH-neh-keh): cabbage-filled dumplings

For Further Reading

Brett, Jan. *The Mitten: A Ukrainian Folktale*. New York: G.P. Putnam's Sons, 1989.

Gosnell, Kelvin. *Belarus, Ukraine, and Moldavia*. Brookfield, Connecticut: The Millbrook Press, 1992.

Kuropas, Myron. *Ukrainians in America*. Minneapolis, Minnesota: Lerner, 1972.

Maxwell, Cassandre. *Yosef's Gift of Many Colors*. Minneapolis, Minnesota: Augsburg Fortress, 1993.

Osborn, Kevin. *Ukrainian Americans*. New York: Chelsea House, 1989.

Index

Page numbers for illustrations are in boldface

About the Author

Rebecca Clay grew up in Sharon, Massachusetts, and received her Bachelor of Science degree from Boston University. In 1982, she began her writing career as a freelance radio correspondent in Paris. Since then, she has written hundreds of public television and radio programs, magazine and newspaper articles, and video scripts.

Ms. Clay is the author of six non-fiction books for children, including *Ties That Bind: Family and Community*, a book about family life in different parts of the world. She has traveled extensively throughout the former Soviet Union. She lives in Pittsboro, North Carolina, with her husband, author/illustrator David Haynes.